Classic Tales

Level 2

The Fisherman and his Wife

Retold by Sue Arengo
Illustrated by Laure Fournier

The Fisherman and his Wife	2
Exercises	20
Picture Dictionary	22
About *Classic Tales*	24

OXFORD
UNIVERSITY PRESS

 A poor fisherman lives in this hut. He lives here with his wife. Every day he goes to the sea.

One day he sees a strange fish. It is strange and beautiful.

'Oh, fisherman! Put me back in the sea!' says the fish. 'I'm not a fish. I'm a magic prince.'

'Oh! ... A magic prince!' says the fisherman. 'We can't eat you.'

He puts the fish back in the sea and he goes home.

'What? No fish!' says his wife. 'Are there no fish in the sea?'

'There's a magic fish,' says the fisherman. 'We can't eat a magic fish … so it's back in the sea.'

'What?' says his wife. 'You silly man! A magic fish can help us. I want something. I want a nice little cottage. Go and ask the fish!'

The fisherman goes back to the sea.

Now the water is green.

The fisherman shouts, 'Oh, magic fish in the sea! Please come up and speak to me.'

'What do you want?' says the fish.

'My wife wants something,' says the fisherman. 'She wants a cottage.'

'Go home!' says the fish. 'She has it.'

Look at this cottage!

The fisherman goes home.

'Look!' says his wife. 'Look at this cottage! This is nice!'

'Yes, Wife!' says the fisherman. 'We can be happy now.'

'Yes,' says his wife. 'Perhaps we can …'

Then she starts to think …

A week later the fisherman's wife says, 'Husband, this cottage is very small. I want something. I want a nice big house.'

'No, Wife, please!' says the fisherman. 'We don't want a big house.'

'Yes, we do,' says his wife. 'Go and ask the fish!'

The fisherman goes back to the sea.

Now the water is purple.

The fisherman shouts, 'Oh, magic fish in the sea! Please come up and speak to me.'

My wife wants a big house.

'What do you want?' says the fish.

'My wife wants something,' says the fisherman. 'She wants a big house.'

'Go home!' says the fish. 'She has it.'

The fisherman goes home.

'Look!' says his wife. 'Look at this house! This is nice!'

'Yes, Wife,' says the fisherman. 'It's very nice. We can be happy now.'

'Yes,' says his wife. 'Perhaps we can …'

Then she starts to think …

A week later the fisherman's wife says, 'Husband, this house is very small. I want something. I want a nice big castle.'

'No, Wife, please!' says the fisherman. 'We don't want a castle.'

'Yes, we do,' says his wife. 'Go and ask the fish!'

The fisherman goes back to the sea.

Now the water is grey.

The fisherman shouts, 'Oh, magic fish in the sea! Please come up and speak to me.'

'What do you want?' says the fish.

'My wife wants something,' says the fisherman. 'She wants a castle.'

'Go home!' says the fish. 'She has it.'

My wife wants a castle.

'This is nice!'

The fisherman goes home.

'Look!' says his wife. 'Look at this castle! This is nice!'

'Yes, Wife,' says the fisherman. 'It's very nice. We can be happy now.'

'Yes,' says his wife. 'Perhaps we can …'

Then she starts to think …

A week later the fisherman's wife says, 'Husband, this castle is very small. I want something. I want a palace … and I want to be queen.'

'No, Wife, please!' says the fisherman. 'We don't want a palace. You don't want to be queen.'

'Yes, I do,' says his wife. 'Go and ask the fish!'

The fisherman goes back to the sea.

Now the water is brown.

The fisherman shouts, 'Oh, magic fish in the sea! Please come up and speak to me.'

'My wife wants to be queen.'

'What do you want?' says the fish.

'My wife wants something,' says the fisherman. 'She wants a palace … and she wants to be queen.'

'Go home!' says the fish. 'She has a palace and she is queen.'

The fisherman goes home.

'Look!' says his wife. 'Look at this palace! I'm the queen. This is nice!'

Look at this palace!

'Yes, Wife,' says the fisherman. 'It's very nice. So now … now, Wife, can we be happy?'

'Yes,' says his wife. 'Perhaps we can …'

Then she starts to think …

The fisherman is tired.

That night he sleeps well … but his wife can't sleep.

'I want … I want … something,' she says.

I want … the world!

It is morning.

'Wake up, Husband!' she says.

'I know what I want. I want … the world! I want to be emperor of all the world.'

'Oh, Wife,' says the fisherman. 'No! You can't have all the world. No one can have all the world. Listen! You are queen. Now be happy!'

'I can't be happy,' cries his wife. 'I can't. I must have all the world. Now go! Go and ask the fish!'

Go and ask the fish!

The fisherman goes back to the sea.

Now the water is black.

The fisherman shouts, 'Oh, magic fish in the sea! Please come up and speak to me.'

'What do you want?' says the fish.

'My wife … wants … something,' says the fisherman. 'She wants the world. She wants … to be emperor … of all the world.'

'Go home,' says the fish. 'And don't come back!'

Go home and don't come back!

The fisherman goes home.

'Look!' says his wife. 'Look at this hut! It isn't very nice … but it's our home.'

Can we be happy now?

Yes, I think we can.

'Yes, Wife,' says the fisherman. 'Can we be happy now?'

The fisherman's wife starts to think …

'Yes,' she says. 'I think we can.'

Exercises

1 Write the words.

1 The fisherman's wife wants a ___cottage___ .

2 A week later she wants a _____ .

3 A week later she wants a _____ .

4 A week later she wants a _____ and she wants to be _____ .

5 The next morning she wants to be emperor of all the _____ .

2 Write the words.

1 (page 3) The fish says it is a magic ___prince___ .
2 (page 7) The fisherman's wife wants a house because the cottage is very _____ .
3 (page 8) The sea is _____ .
4 (page 16) The fisherman sleeps well because he is _____ .
5 (page 18) The sea is _____ .

3 Match and write the words.

1 a ___blue___ fish
2 a _____ castle
3 a _____ sea
4 a _____ fisherman
5 a _____ queen
6 a _____ house

4 Write the numbers and write the words.

fish   hut   cottage   ~~sea~~   castle   home

☐ I want a nice big _____.
[1] Oh, magic fish in the ___sea___!
☐ Go _____ and don't come back!
☐ Go and ask the _____!
☐ Look at this _____. It isn't very nice, but it's our home.
☐ Look at this _____!

21

Picture Dictionary

castle

grey

cottage

house

emperor

husband

fish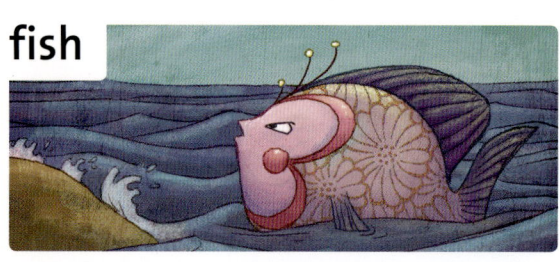

hut

fisherman

palace

poor *He is poor.*

prince

purple

queen

sea

shout

sleep

think

tired *He is tired.*

wake up

wife

world

Classic Tales

Classic stories retold for learners of English – bringing the magic of traditional storytelling to the language classroom

Level 1: 100 headwords
- The Enormous Turnip
- The Little Red Hen
- Lownu Mends the Sky
- The Magic Cooking Pot
- Mansour and the Donkey
- Peach Boy
- The Princess and the Pea
- Rumplestiltskin
- The Shoemaker and the Elves
- Three Billy-Goats

Level 2: 150 headwords
- Amrita and the Trees
- Big Baby Finn
- The Fisherman and his Wife
- The Gingerbread Man
- Jack and the Beanstalk
- Thumbelina
- The Town Mouse and the Country Mouse
- The Ugly Duckling

Level 3: 200 headwords
- Aladdin
- Goldilocks and the Three Bears
- The Little Mermaid
- Little Red Riding Hood

Level 4: 300 headwords
- Cinderella
- The Goose Girl
- Sleeping Beauty
- The Twelve Dancing Princesses

Level 5: 400 headwords
- Beauty and the Beast
- The Magic Brocade
- Pinocchio
- Snow White and the Seven Dwarfs

All *Classic Tales* have an accompanying
- **e-Book with Audio Pack** containing the book and the e-book with audio, for use on a computer or CD player. Teachers can also project the e-book onto an interactive whiteboard to use it like a Big Book.
- **Activity Book and Play** providing extra language practice and the story adapted as a play for performance in class or on stage.

For more details, visit
www.oup.com/elt/readers/classictales

OXFORD
UNIVERSITY PRESS

Great Clarendon Street, Oxford OX2 6DP

Oxford University Press is a department of the University of Oxford. It furthers the University's objective of excellence in research, scholarship, and education by publishing worldwide in

Oxford New York

Auckland Cape Town Dar es Salaam Hong Kong Karachi
Kuala Lumpur Madrid Melbourne Mexico City Nairobi
New Delhi Shanghai Taipei Toronto

With offices in

Argentina Austria Brazil Chile Czech Republic France Greece
Guatemala Hungary Italy Japan Poland Portugal Singapore
South Korea Switzerland Thailand Turkey Ukraine Vietnam

OXFORD and OXFORD ENGLISH are registered trade marks of Oxford University Press in the UK and in certain other countries

This edition © Oxford University Press 2011

The moral rights of the author have been asserted

Database right Oxford University Press (maker)

First published in Classic Tales 2001

2015 2014 2013 2012 2011
10 9 8 7 6 5 4 3 2 1

No unauthorized photocopying

All rights reserved. No part of this publication may be reproduced, stored in a retrieval system, or transmitted, in any form or by any means, without the prior permission in writing of Oxford University Press, or as expressly permitted by law, or under terms agreed with the appropriate reprographics rights organization. Enquiries concerning reproduction outside the scope of the above should be sent to the ELT Rights Department, Oxford University Press, at the address above

You must not circulate this book in any other binding or cover and you must impose this same condition on any acquirer

Any websites referred to in this publication are in the public domain and their addresses are provided by Oxford University Press for information only. Oxford University Press disclaims any responsibility for the content

ISBN: 978 0 19 423902 8

This *Classic Tale* title is available as an e-Book with Audio Pack
ISBN: 978 0 19 423905 9

Also available: The Fisherman and his Wife Activity Book and Play
ISBN: 978 0 19 423903 5

Printed in China

This book is printed on paper from certified and well-managed sources.

ACKNOWLEDGEMENTS

Illustrated by: Laure Fournier / The Organisation